Bilston, Bradley & Ladymoor

A Second Selection

J.R. Walters' music shop was in High Street, opposite Dudley Street. Its main feature was a large glass-fronted window where pianos and other musical instruments were displayed to their best advantage, but 78 records and sheet music were the best sellers. The shop closed in about 1975. (*Author*)

Bilston, Bradley & Ladymoor

A Second Selection

RON DAVIES

SUTTON PUBLISHING

Sutton Publishing Limited
Phoenix Mill · Thrupp · Stroud
Gloucestershire · GL5 2BU

First published 2002

Reprinted in 2002

Half-title: Advertising in the early 1920s was certainly not high tech, but it served its purpose. Here Professor Wood makes sure everyone is aware of the films showing at his Town Hall cinema. The blanketed driver of the horse and trap is James Joseph. (*Angela Bird*)

Title page: This photograph shows our oldest known local inhabitant – a spider-like creature that was found near Ladymoor in an ironstone nodule. It was probably common in all three areas represented in this book, if not throughout the whole of the Black Country. It was a creature of the carboniferous age, some 300 million years ago. This specimen is now housed in the Natural History Museum.

British Library Cataloguing in Publication Data
A catalogue record for this book is available from the British Library.

ISBN 0-7509-2947-2

Typeset in 10.5/13.5 Photina.
Typesetting and origination by
Sutton Publishing Limited.
Printed and bound in England by
J.H. Haynes & Co. Ltd, Sparkford.

THE BLACK COUNTRY SOCIETY

This voluntary society, affiliated to the Civic Trust, was founded in 1967 as a reaction to the trend of the late 1950s and early 1960s to amalgamate everything into large units and in the Midlands to sweep away the area's industrial heritage in the process.

The general aim of the Society is to create interest in the past, present and future of the Black Country, and early on it campaigned for the establishment of an industrial museum. In 1975 the Black Country Living Museum was started by Dudley Borough Council on 26 acres of totally derelict land adjoining the grounds of Dudley Castle. This has developed into an award-winning museum which attracts over 250,000 visitors annually.

In 1998 the Museum Board secured a lottery grant of nearly £3 million towards the £4.5 million cost of building a state-of-the-art interpretation centre. Known as the Rolfe Street Baths Project as it incorporated that Smethwick building which was transferred to the museum site, it was officially opened on 18 May 2001. It includes two fine exhibition halls, administration and storage rooms and retains the original Victorian building's façade. The museum's already wide range of attractions is likely soon to be increased in the field of transport with the acquisition of two major collections of vehicles.

At the Black Country Living Museum there is a boat dock fully equipped to restore narrowboats of wood and iron and different vessels can be seen on the dock throughout the year. From behind the Bottle and Glass Inn visitors can travel on a canal boat into Dudley Canal Tunnel, a memorable journey to see spectacular limestone caverns and the fascinating Castle Mill Basin.

There are 2,650 members of the Black Country Society and all receive the quarterly magazine *The Blackcountryman*, of which 136 issues have been published since its founding in 1967. In the whole collection there are some 2,000 authoritative articles on all aspects of the Black Country by historians, teachers, researchers, students, subject experts and ordinary folk with an extraordinary story to tell. The whole constitutes a unique resource about the area and is a mine of information for students and researchers who frequently refer to it. Many schools and libraries are subscribers. Over 3,300 copies of the magazine are printed each quarter. It is non-commercial, and contributors do not receive payment for their articles.

PO Box 71 · Kingswinford · West Midlands DY6 9YN

CONTENTS

Bilston football ground, 1912. Among those on the front row are Sid and Harold Wootton. (*Arthur Wootton*)

Map of Bilston, Bradley and Ladymoor. (*Ron Davies*)

INTRODUCTION

The history of Bilston goes back many centuries, though the name first comes to light in the Anglo-Saxon charters of 994. Here we find *Bilsetnatun*. *Setna* meant a settler or inhabitant, so therefore we have 'The town of Bil's folk'. But why would anyone want to settle here in the first place? There is scant evidence that the Romans ever came to the area, though their road from London to Birkenhead passed through what is now Bilston Town. The Iron Age ancients may have found a niche here, for the noted Bilston stone was a useful sharpening material, invaluable for producing an edge on iron tools. Domesday Book offers no evidence of stone quarrying. It simply states: 'Bilston belongs to the King, it has 2 hides of land, and land for 4 ploughs. There are 8 villagers and 3 smallholders with 3 ploughs. Meadow, 1 acre; woodland ½ league long and ½ wide. The value was 20s; now 30s.'

Dr Robert Plot in his *Natural History of Staffordshire* (1686) gives the first written evidence of stone quarrying here. He states: 'The quarry at Bilston is very remarkable, it lying in beds *in Plano Horizontis*, one under another, 12 beds deep, every bed being thicker than that above it an inch or more, so that the lower bed is about a yard thick, of which they make troughs, cisterns etc, some of the tables of stone rising so large and even that Mr Hoo of Bradley got one here 8 yards long, naturally so very even that in the whole length it did not bevel or depart from a true level above an inch.' The last organisation to make use of the stone was the Cannon Ironworks, Deepfields, which made grindstones of various sizes.

During the Tudor period timbered mansions were dotted around Bilston. Church Street in particular had a wealth of such properties and the last of these was demolished in the late 1950s. The only remaining proof of the antiquity of the town is seen in the Greyhound and Punchbowl Inn, in High Street.

Probably the most important phase in our history was the advent of the industrial age. It was Cumberland-born John Wilkinson (1728–1808) whose inventiveness and astonishing enterprise helped most of all to develop the innate mineral wealth and resources of the area. His work was paralleled by development in other trades, helping to establish that wide variety of industries that became a feature of the town. The population of Bilston was 1,004 in 1695 but had jumped to 5,600 by 1801, and by 1953 it was 33,420. Bradley and Ladymoor were both born as a result of their extensive mineral deposits, but in

Bradley the natural resources brought the development of many ironworks while in Ladymoor mines came to dominate. Today Bradley's ironworks are no more; it is largely residential with a few surrounding industries. Ladymoor has both residential areas and light industrial works.

Through photographs and the odd sketch or painting this book documents our industrial and social heritage, and I hope you enjoy this second volume as much as the first.

Ron Davies and Roy Hawthorne, the authors of *Bilston, Bradley & Ladymoor*, the first book in this series, would like to express their thanks to all who are pictured in these photographs for sparing the time to attend what we believe was Bilston's first ever book launch. It was enormously successful and raised £500 for Compton Hospice, with royalties to follow as sales of the book continue. Thanks also to all who purchased the book from other sources.

1

Bilston

A Charter Day souvenir programme commemorating Bilston's becoming a borough in 1933. The background is a capital 'B', which may stand either for 'Bilston' or 'Borough', and on it are the year, month and day of the Charter. The rays represent the rising sun that topped the crest on the new coat of arms. The lower border shows swineherds' huts, perhaps suggesting Bilston's earliest industry, pig-keeping. The upper border, which has been badly worn over the years, represents the blast furnaces for which Bilston was known.

The first Mayor, or Charter Mayor, of Bilston was Councillor Herbert Beach JP, who ran a family furnishing business in High Street. Herbert was devoted to Bilston and its inhabitants, and often visited the local schools, not to teach but to put across what a great little town Bilston was and to encourage the children to be proud of its new borough status. (*Charter Day Souvenir Programme*)

The Charter Mayoress was Miss G. Beach, presumably Mayor Beach's daughter. (*Charter Day Souvenir Programme*)

Members of Bilston Urban District Council, 1933. Back row, left to right: J. Wells MRCP, J. Toole CC, J. Winyard. Middle row: G.H. Plant, J.E. Downs, J. Roberts, Mrs H. Holland JP, H. Homfray, J.T. Baker, S. Hague JP, W. Leighton. Front row: T.R. Wood JP, CC, W.T. Fellows JP, Vice Chairman, H. Beach JP, Chairman, W.M. Hughes. (*Charter Day Souvenir Programme*)

Chief officers of the council, 1933. Back row, left to right: G.L. Kirk (Collector), J.S. Colbourne (Education Secretary), E.J. Aldridge (Rating and Valuation Officer), T.H. Aston (Librarian). Middle row: T.S. Price (Waterworks Manager), W.G. Lofthouse ARIBA (Architect), H.E. Carder (Financial Officer), F. Barnett (Sanitary Inspector), G. Jones (Estate Manager). Front row: H.W. Keartland (Treasurer), A.F.B. Sidwick MIM and CE (Surveyor and Waterworks Engineer), Joseph L. Arlidge (Clerk and Solicitor), B.C. Haller MA, LRCP, DPH (Medical Officer of Health and School Medical Officer), T.W.W. Skemp (Deputy Clerk). (*Charter Day Souvenir Programme*)

The Right Honourable, the Earl of Harrowby, Lord Lieutenant of Staffordshire, who brought the Charter to Bilston and presented it to the Charter Mayor in Hickman Park. (*Charter Day Souvenir Programme*)

The Deputy Charter Mayor, Councillor Thomas Reay Wood JP, CC, who besides being involved in politics was also the entertainment guru in the town. (*Charter Day Souvenir Programme*)

Two early nineteenth-century Bilston tokens. The token marked 'payable by Rushbury and Woolley' is a mystery. The Woolleys were an old Bilston family and one Edward Woolley owned a screw factory at the rear of the schools in Prosser Street. He was known as Screw Woolley and was an acquaintance of George Rushbury, a landowner who had some great influence in the town. John Freeman in his *Black Country Sketches* (1931) mentions the token and the fact that Rushbury and Woolley met regularly at the Bull's Head Hotel in High Street. There is no mention, however, of an industrial partnership, although there must have been one. (*Stan Hill*)

Samuel Fereday had two tokens minted. The one pictured here is rather plain but his other token shows his furnaces at Priestfield. He was also one of the larger landowners in the town, and a trustee of John Wilkinson's Bradley estate. He later became bankrupt and ended his days in France. Most local tradesmen refused to acknowledge these tokens as being of intrinsic value. The silver token at the top of the page was only worth eightpence farthing, and the Fereday token just over a halfpenny. The Priestfield furnaces are depicted on page 19. (*Author*)

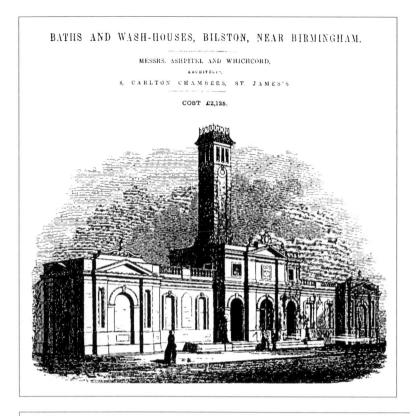

BATHS AND WASH-HOUSES, BILSTON, NEAR BIRMINGHAM.

MESSRS. ASHPITEL AND WHICHCORD,
ARCHITECTS,
8, CARLTON CHAMBERS, ST. JAMES'S

COST £2,125.

Bilston Baths originally stood on the corner of Bath Street and Market Street. They opened in 1853 but by 1892 were in a state of collapse. However, by 1895 they had been considerably improved and the classical façade was still intact. They fell into disuse soon after the last war, and the building ended its days as a small chrome plating factory. (*Stan Hill*)

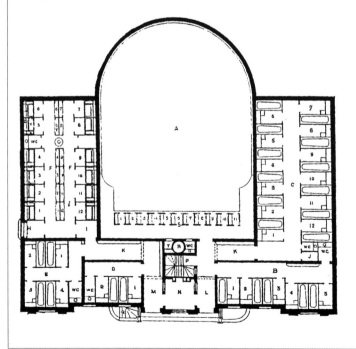

A. Swimming-bath
B. Five men's baths—first class.
C. Twelve men's baths—second class.
D. Two women's baths—first class.
E. Four women's baths—second class.
F F. Wash-house, twelve compartments.
G. Wringing machine.
H. Entrance to Wash-house.
I. Office.
J. Soap, &c.
K. Lobby.
L. Men's entrance.
M. Women's entrance.
N. Office.
P. Bath-keeper's entrance.
Q. To the stokery.
R. Chimney-shaft.
S. Dressing-boxes.
T. Urinal.
V. Wash-tub.
W. Boiling-tub.
X. Rinsing-tub.
Y. Drying-closet.
Z. Dripping-board.

This plan of the old baths shows their features. They were demolished in the mid-1960s. (*Stan Hill*)

Swan Bank, 1980. Next to Newey Bros electrical shop and a tiny stores is the Swan Bank Tavern, or Blazing Stump as it is popularly known. Many have offered accounts of how the Blazing Stump acquired its name, but one story goes that a former licensee with a wooden leg fell asleep by the open fire. The leg then overheated and started to burn. (*Jack Smith*)

Overleaf: This impressive 1920s photograph of Bilston Town Hall really captures the mood of the time. Professor Wood is advertising his Town Hall cinema shows, a horse and trap is waiting outside the main entrance, and people are standing around in anticipation, probably waiting for some important figure to emerge from the building. The tram advertises Fazenda Coffee on its side, and on the rear, George E. Brown promotes his ranges, grates and chimney pieces. (Brown had an ironmonger's business on Snow Hill, Wolverhampton.) On the left a tobacconist advertises the brands of the day. How long would the huge gas lamps last in this day and age? (*Black Country Society*)

One of the few pubs with character left in the town is the Spread Eagle in Lichfield Street, seen here in 1980. Next door to it is a rather small building that has seen a large variety of uses in its time. At present it is incorporated into the Spread Eagle complex, but within living memory it has served as a toilet facility and a tramway waiting room. (*Author*)

The interior of the small building mentioned above, *c.* 1900. It was once the town jail, while way back in the early nineteenth century a family named Salter flourished here making springs and spring balances. They later removed to West Bromwich, and today they are nationwide suppliers of electronic scales, weigh bridges and other equipment. (*The Bilston Almanac*)

This simple black and white enamel is in the collection of Bantock House Museum, which is noted for its Bilston enamels. Stating simply 'A Trifle from Bilston', it shows the building that was 'Samuel Proud's Asylum'. Its site is a bit of a mystery, though John Price in his *Story of Bilston* (page 33) says: 'Prouds Lane was called after Major Proud, the proprietor of a lunatic asylum at Ivy House, at the corner of Wellington Road and Mount Pleasant.' (*The Wolverhampton Antiquary*, *June 1937*)

This well-known building on the corner of Wellington Road and Prouds Lane, now a community facility, was formerly the Centre Health Clinic. Nikolaus Pevsner in his *Buildings of Staffordshire* states simply: 'By Lyons, Israel and Ellis 1938–39. It is small, light brick and horizontal windows, the moment of Dudok inspiration in England.' The clinic was very well placed, standing as it did at the heart of various doctors' and dentists' surgeries. (*Ron Davies Collection*)

Dr Dan Sullivan in practice, *c.* 1960. The patient is Mr K. Duckett. Dr Dan Sullivan started practice with Dr Wells in Caledonia Street in 1921. He later had his own surgery built in Dover Street, where he was joined by Dr Barry in 1951. Dr Peter Sullivan joined the practice in 1960 when Dr Sullivan semi–retired through ill health. When Dr Barry passed away Dr Peter Sullivan was joined by Dr Rangel who now carries on the practice. Dr Peter Sullivan retired in 1995. (*I. Duckett*)

Dr Barry, probably writing out a prescription, *c.* 1965. (*I. Duckett*)

Dr Peter Sullivan, *c.* 1990. (*I. Duckett*)

Dr Rangel in a relaxed pose,
c. 1995. (*I. Duckett*)

Mrs I. Duckett joined the
practice as receptionist/
secretary in 1952 intending to
stay for three months. She
retired forty-five years later in
1995. This is Mrs Duckett at
her desk. She had lots of
memories of her clientele,
especially the Monday
morning regulars. However, on
one particular Monday a
certain Mary failed to turn up.
The following week she was
asked why she had not turned
up, to which she replied, 'I was
poorly last Monday and
couldn't get here!' (*I. Duckett*)

Bilston Girls High School was built in the 1930s. The old pit mounds of the Wellington Road were levelled and gracious lawns and avenues of flowering trees were created. Who would not want their daughters to be educated in this choice setting? Today the building stands forlorn. Its windows are blocked, its future uncertain. (*Author*)

For a long time this building on the Wellington Road was Edge's shoe manufactory, though its features show that it had earlier served as Hall Park Brewery. Richard Harper was both the brewer here and licensee of the adjacent New Bull's Head. He also owned a number of public houses in the town. Today it serves as a fashion factory under the title Shri Durga Bhawan. This photograph was taken in 1980. (*Author*)

This sign was once located on the Wellington Road in Hall Park on the footpath close to the fence of the house adjacent to Biddlestone's Furnishers. It stated simply 'High Level Station 2 Miles' and pointed to nowhere in particular. The sign must have been placed there during a period of competition with Wolverhampton Low Level station. The High Level station served the London Midland & Scottish Railway which was running by about 1840. The Great Western Railway served the Low Level station and came later in about 1854. The cast iron sign, an important town artefact, disappeared soon after this photograph was taken in about 1975. (*Author*)

As was mentioned on page 11, Samuel Fereday had two penny tokens minted, one with a simple obverse as shown and the other with a view of his Priestfield furnaces, from which this drawing was taken. A William Ward later took over the furnaces and gave his name to Ward Street, which runs where the furnaces were situated. (*Author*)

Just a short walk away from the heart of Bilston town is Peascroft Wood in Mountford Lane just off Mount Pleasant. It was created some 100 years ago on an old pit mound to enclose the Bilston fever hospital. Soon after the Second World War the hospital closed and was taken down. The wood and its adjacent meadow came under the wing of the Bilston Conservation Association, but since the organisation's demise the wood had become much neglected. This is how it looked in 1985. (*Author*)

A group of girls studying in one of the quieter rooms in Bilston library, *c.* 1955. (*Ron Davies Collection*)

Bevan's dairy farm was situated on the corner of the Willenhall and Moseley Roads. Pit banks were the main feature of this area until about 1930, but if coal was the first priority in people's lives here, milk was the second, for the miners were careful to leave certain meadows clear for the grazing of cattle. There was no such thing as bottled, pasteurised, sterilised or skimmed milk in those days. Folk either had to fetch it or wait until it was delivered, usually by hand cart or pony and trap and straight out of the churn. (*Author*)

The former George & Crown public house in Moseley Road, opposite Bevan's dairy farm, was demolished to make way for the present building in the late 1920s. The new pub was built to cater for residents of the new estates that were beginning to spring up. The little cottage to the right of the pub was the home of Rosehannah Harrison and the incline to the side of the cottage led to the meadow where Mr Beven grazed his cattle. (*Author*)

To the rear of the George & Crown lay Hadley's brickworks, or the Brickill as it was called – short for brick kiln. As these two photographs show, it was a rather large site. It closed in about 1980. (*Author*)

Moseley Road was a long and lonely lane in days past with just the odd cottage to break the monotony. During the nineteenth century it was known as Throttle Goose Lane, perhaps a corruption of Throstle Gorse Lane, as gorse was once plentiful hereabouts, as were thrushes. The cottage, pictured in about 1935, was the home of Joe Pooler and family. Its garden harboured a Tettenhal Dick pear tree that in autumn produced small sweet pears which you could buy for a penny a capful. Such trees are still to be found in the area. (*Author*)

This old building, which I believe to have been a miner's cot, came to light in about 1987 when a copse of trees was cut down in a rather large garden on the east side of Moseley Road. It appears to have been used as a pigeon loft. Sadly it had deteriorated too far to be saved. (*Author*)

Bilston carnival, 1930. This rare photograph shows the procession coming round from Beckett Street into Queen Street, with the carnival queen and her attendants on a trailer being towed by a solid-tyred Ferguson-type tractor. Note the corner shop to the right of the houses, then on the very fringe of Bilston town. The Queen Street Garage, with its Belfast roof, dominates the scene with its advertisements. At that time almost no one had a radio, yet the garage was already advertising that it could charge accumulators, one of contemporary radio sets' main power supplies. (*Wolverhampton Archives and Local Studies*)

It was into such a scene as the one shown above that little Dot Slaney (née Beech), all dressed up in her Scottish trappings, aspired to go. (*Dot Slaney*)

St Mary's Church, Oxford Street, early 1930s. The Bilston Brook flows to Darlaston to meet the River Tame there. To the left of the brook the ground was strewn with slag from Price's blast furnace which once stood here. On 3 August 1832 the first case of the Asian cholera in Bilston occurred here. At that time the brook was a canal serving the furnace. It led to the Walsall–Birmingham canal at Darlaston. Bilston football ground is to the right of the scene. (*Author*)

What a difference forty years make. This is Oxford Street in 1970. The buildings belonged to James Wilkes Printers which closed in about 1982. (*Roy Hawthorne*)

Church Street from the Town Hall, *c.* 1950. On the left are Chapman's cake shop and Forrester's furnishing department. (*F.A. Barnett Collection*)

There don't appear to have been many follies in Bilston (follies are simply fanciful structures of no practical use, usually found on landed estates) but this one, photographed in February 1991, turned up when some old shops adjacent to the Town Hall in Church Street were demolished. The area is now a quiet spot with a bench. The Gothic-style structure was an early nineteenth-century creation of furnace slag, ironstone and Bilston stone, and not a long forgotten medieval church remnant, so it was demolished and we lost perhaps 200 years of Bilston's industrial past. There is another folly in Bilston, known as Dryden's Tower. However, the Bilston in question is located just to the south of Edinburgh. (*Author*)

This old cottage known as 'The Retreat' stands cheek by jowl with St Leonard's Church. It was formerly the home of Bilston's nineteenth-century saint, John Etheridge. A little information about him says: 'He was a deeply religious man but of no particular church. He had a little school of his own where he taught miners to read the scriptures. He had a humble bookshop selling bibles etc.; his counter was the savings bank and clothing club of the district. He worked unstintingly to help the cholera victims of 1832 and 1849. When he died on October 28 1856 aged 84, 15,000 Bilstonians followed his funeral. The last words he said were, "Lord now lettest thou thy servant depart in peace".'

Walsall Street, 1980. Only the shop names have changed here in the last twenty years. This corner shop was a florist's run by Knight & Brown and today it is a chemist's. (*Jack Smith*)

Woolridge's confectioners, bakers and grocers, 1961. The shop stood on the corner of Church Street and Stafford Street, and the staff were posing here for a photograph to commemorate Evelyn Smith's fifty years' service. Left to right: Lucy Hughes, Evelyn Smith, Vi Grainger, Edith Henderson and Pat Hughes. (*Vi Grainger*)

Evelyn Smith is seen here posing by her trusty slicing machine. The shop closed for business in about 1976. (*Vi Grainger*)

Like it or hate it, one has to admire the workmanship and thought that went into creating this mesmerising bronze sculpture. It represents the working women not only of Bilston, but also of the Black Country as a whole. The sculpture called *Women's Work* supposedly depicts a local pit bank lass or coal picker. It is difficult to put every aspect of the work they did into one sculpture, for in the old days – and not so old days – there were ladies of the brickill and foundry core makers, they worked on dangerous presses and war saw them employed as welders and oxyacetylene cutters. In the older days they competed with the men; they wore flat caps, smoked clay pipes and probably swore like them too. The sculpture by Rose Garrard of Malvern was unveiled on Friday 6 March 1998 by Clare Short, Birmingham MP and Secretary of State for International Development. (*Author*)

Looking north up Church Street on a hot summer's day, *c.* 1950. Awnings kept shop interiors cool. The shadowed building on the left was the former market hall. I don't know who the person in white on a bicycle was but the one behind him with a basket on his handlebars was yours truly. (*Andrew Barnett Collection*)

The Market Tavern in Church Street, 1975. Note the bicycle parked outside – it's just not done these days. (*Black Country Society*)

The façade of Bilston market looking worse for wear, *c.* 1967. Built in 1891, it closed in 1970 and was really missed by the older generation. It was cold in the winter, but it was a shoppers' paradise. Goods ranged from meat to china, from greens to music – the variety was endless. It was always busy, always boisterous, a wonderful market. (*Ron Arnold*)

Here is real nostalgia – a rare view of the back of the market, *c.* 1967. If the indoor market was special, the outdoor market was even more so. Here were the lino men, fish men from Grimsby, quack doctors, conjurers, ventriloquists, escapologists, tipsters – it was theatre royal. The old marketeers may have vanished but the present market still attracts the large crowds. However, there is no real nostalgia. (*Ron Arnold*)

Bilston firemen, with two members demonstrating their oxygen equipment, *c.* 1950. Left to right: Len ?, Horace Hawkins, Roland Summers (of the Crown Inn, Bank Street, Bradley), Bert Wilkes, Bob Slaney, -?-, -?-. (*Dot Slaney*)

Bilston firemen parading in the Summer Hill Road area of Coseley, where they were always welcome, 1950. (*Dot Slaney*)

This 1930s advertisement indicates types of work Bottom Sankey's was capable of carrying out. In order to survive, the firm produced even smaller items like brush and pan sets, beetle traps, culinary equipment and stainless steel ware for hospitals – the list of such commodities was endless. Bottom Sankey's consisted of Albert Street works and Bath Street works, both now gone. Top Sankey's or Bankfield works in Bradley is still in production. (*Staffordshire County Handbook, 1935*)

Day trips from Joseph Sankey's were always popular with the workforce. A few of the names of those in the group are known. Back row, left to right: -?-, Bill Langston, Sidney Pearson, Frank Greaves, -?-, -?-, -?-, Lol Rogers, -?-, -?-. Middle row: Eric Cole is second from the left; the names of the others are not known. Front row: -?-, George Butler, -?-, Joe Poole, -?-, -?-, -?-, Horace Butler, ? Howell, Ray Hickman, -?-, -?-. The photograph was taken in the 1950s. (*Arthur Wootton*)

Joseph Sankey's probably had the most dedicated St John Ambulance staff of any company in the area. This group poses with great pride. Their mentor was one of Bilston's foremost general practitioners, Dr Lambah. Back row, left to right: B. Middleton, -?-, -?-, Arthur Wootton, -?-, -?-, -?-, -?-, Harold Hammond, -?-, F. Greaves, -?-, -?-, J. Gammon, Norman Fellows, -?-. Third row: Rose Cole, -?-, E. Bott, Rose Hickinbottom, -?-, -?-, -?-, -?-, -?-, -?-, -?-, -?-, -?-, -?-, -?-, Mrs A. Pearson, Mrs Bryan, -?-, -?-, Ms Bott. Second row: -?-, L.O. Neil, -?-, C. Beddow, G. Hughes, Miss Shackleton, Mr Peel, Dr Lambah, A. Perry, A. White, F. Alexander, -?-, -?-, Fred Coburn, Percy Maydew. Front row: B. Bott, T. Whitfield, E. Smith, -?-, -?-, C. Smith. The photograph was taken in about 1940. (*Arthur Wootton*)

Posing with their hard-won shields in about 1940, these members of the Sankey St John Ambulance group are: standing, left to right: G. Hughes, -?-, C. Mills, Bernard Broadhurst, C.T. Peel. Seated: -?-, Percy Maydew, Jim Bromley. (*Arthur Wootton*)

This is another winning team from the Sankey Division posing with the Burton Shield, won in the first round of the St John Ambulance national competition, *c*. 1940. Standing, left to right: Ted Whitfield, Fred Alexander. Seated: Jack Kelsey, Sgt White, Percy Maydew. (*Arthur Wootton*)

Members of the St John Ambulance enjoying a break from duty, *c*. 1940. Left to right: George Hughes, Arthur Wootton, Percy Maydew, Bernard Broadhurst. (*Arthur Wootton*)

Looking down the Bankfield Road, *c.* 1993. Sankey's Bath Street works (now Morrison's supermarket) are on the left and Albert Street works are on the right. Note the bridge in the distance connecting the two works. Sankey's Top Works are on the horizon. Only the trees now remain to mark the site of this once vibrant company. (*Author*)

The main gates that once led into the heart of the great Bath Street works, *c.* 1993. The barriers went up and the earth was piled up to keep out travellers. The site is now still after all its labours. Soon Sankey's would all just be a memory. (*Author*)

Looking up the Bankfield Road, with a view of the Albert Street works, *c.* 1994. Nobody worked there any more. The cars were parked outside the Sankey Social Club, which was soon to close too. (*Author*)

Soon after the picture at the top of the page was taken the scene was one of total destruction. It marked the end of a 140-year era for the works. You may note the travellers were quick to move into the scene. There were rich pickings for them here. (*Author*)

A last look at some of the goods produced by Sankey's soon after the Second World War. This is a domestic paraffin heater. They were very popular for a while but there were fears that they were dangerous. (*George Stevens*)

This is a different type of heater, a cooker in fact. This model was not welcome in ordinary household kitchens, but found its way to isolated farmhouses, or was exported to countries lacking gas and electricity supplies. (*George Stevens*)

Not many photographs of old Dudley Street have survived. This one, taken in about 1980, shows the last building left standing in a once busy street. The Hop Pole was kept by the Draisey family for many years. (*Black Country Society*)

Between Dudley Street and Capponfield, *c.* 1985. The earth removers had just levelled the land to accommodate the new Black Country Route, but at the last moment the line of the road was switched to its present position nearer to the town. Through the gap Capponfield House can be seen. The embankments once carried the old Worcester & Wolverhampton Railway and the Great Western Railway. The prominent factory building belongs to Metabrasives Ltd. This was once the site of Barbor's Field furnaces and for many years after it was covered with slag heaps and pit waste mounds. Today the area is covered with maturing woodlands and open grassy rides. It is said to be earmarked for development as an urban village. (*Author*)

In Market Street, opposite Sankey's Albert Street works, stood the complex of St Luke's. The old school with all its associated memories had gone by the late 1960s and the church was soon to follow. Its tower is seen in the background of this photograph taken in about 1938. The spire was found to be unsafe and was removed. (*Ron Davies Collection*)

Dudley Street, looking west down Prosser Street, *c*. 1985. Tomstore was a small steel fabricating business. Formerly a row of old houses occupied the site. The next building along was once Stonefield Baptist Chapel. On redundancy it became an ice-cream factory run by Don Taylor, whose family had a confectionery, ice-cream and newspaper shop in High Street. Next to the old chapel was Stonefield House and the last building in the street belonged to Wilde's the builders. Prosser Street took its name from the Revd W. Prosser who was the incumbent at St Luke's Church at the end of the nineteenth and beginning of the twentieth centuries. (*Author*)

The popular Greyhound and Punchbowl Inn in High Street, 1980s. It was known as Stowheath Manor in about 1457. It is the last of its kind in the town, which once abounded with these octagonal-style buildings occupied by the local gentry. Octagonal actually meant having eight gables, but sadly only five now remain, four of which are seen in this view. The building is certainly a long way from Stowheath but the original manor house lay between the Wolverhampton–Bilston road and the Wolverhampton–Willenhall road in Chillington Lane. The Chillington furnaces were built on the site of the old moated house. (*Black Country Society*)

The manor house as it was at the end of the eighteenth and beginning of the nineteenth centuries. The drawing shows what was then the eastern elevation. Today that elevation is just a plain brick wall, the gables and extension having been removed to allow the building of the shops which still remain on the site. (*Author*)

Pitt's butcher's shop, corner of High Street and Hartshorn Street, early 1920s. The family had been established in the shop since at least 1900 when a John Pitt was the butcher. Left to right: Reg, Gwen, Brenda and Eric Pitt. Note the little boy getting in on the act on the right. The premises today are far removed from butchering, having served as a popular car accessories store for the last quarter of a century. (*Andy Patel*)

(*Opposite above*): On the opposite side of the High Street from the Greyhound pub, there were some old-established shops, including a furniture and a cabinet-making business run by the Beach family since 1824. However, the year 2000 saw its demise. For many years it was run by Herbert Beach, who was elected as Bilston's first mayor in 1933. (*Author*)

(*Opposite below*): Adjacent to Beach's shop was the little pub called The Royal Exchange, now better known as The Trumpet. It is a popular venue for lovers of live jazz music. Next door is the High Street sub-post office, without its current mock-Tudor effect when this picture was taken in about 1980. (*Black Country Society*)

Further along High Street, on the other side of the once merging Stonefield Walk and Stonefield Road, lay Oatmeal Square. It is said that Scottish emigrant workers once resided in this vicinity. This photograph, taken in about 1980, shows a little of the area and the former Golden Cup public house, which was also once popular for jazz music. Next to it is Whitfield's corn and gardening shop. This little area of the town was full of character before the Second World War. Stonefield Walk had a row of old houses; Stonefield Road had Comer's vehicle body building workshops; a little nook set between Comer's and the shops in Oatmeal Square contained a blacksmith's forge where horses were shod – the pungent smell of burning hooves is something that stays with you for ever. In the triangle formed by Stonefield Walk and Stonefield Road stood Winyard's wood manufactory. (*Black Country Society*)

High Street showing The Trumpet, the post office, The Golden Cup and Whitfield's shop, now turned into a Chinese take-away, *c.* 1987. The fine building housing Apollo and Motor Junction was for many years a high-class furniture shop belonging to a Sammy Dale. (*Author*)

High Street, *c.* 1987. The Plough Inn once occupied the building with the hoarding and to its right is The Swan, which is still in business. In between the two buildings an opening led to a caravan site and the former Swan Boxing Booth. The whole site, except The Swan, is now occupied by one new building housing Lidl's supermarket, Co-op chemist and the Town Housing Office. (*Author*)

Looking west from Prosser Street, *c.* 1975. The car scrapyard is dominated in the background by the Elisabeth furnace. (*Author*)

Like the Hop Pole in Dudley Street, The Union pub in Coseley Road was to end its days in complete isolation. Like The Swan in High Street The Union had a boxing booth – standing room only – in the 1930s. It is seen here in 1990. (*Author*)

Coseley Road railway bridge with The Union pub in the distance, 1970. The embankment on the left carried a private railway line into the steelworks. At the end of the embankment, although you cannot see it in this view, stood another bridge under which Tarmac steam lorries plied to and fro to a huge slag heap, so huge in fact that a road spiralled around it to the top. (*Harry Eccleston*)

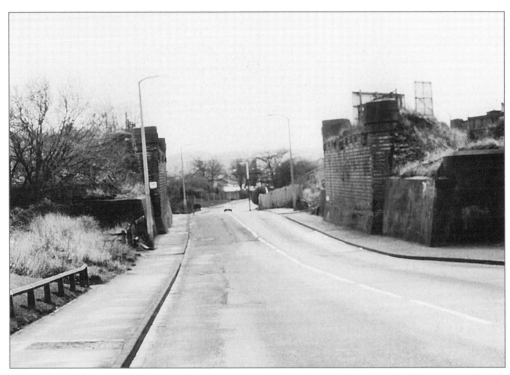

The remains of Coseley Road railway bridge looking towards Broadlanes and Ladymoor, 1990. Just past the bridge on the right is the road that went under the second bridge, the top of which is just visible on the far right. (*Author*)

The Hand and Keys public house at the head of Wolverhampton Street, 1980. It was becoming redundant as so many pubs have here in recent years, but the buildings look in great condition. Since demolition in 1987 the site has remained derelict. (*Black Country Society*)

Almost opposite the Hand and Keys stood St Michael's mission church. The original building was taken down because of structural defects but with the promise that a new one would replace it. Here work on the new building is in progress in about 1980 away from the avenue of popular trees that had undermined the foundations of the old one. The poplar trees were planted to commemorate the local fallen of the First World War. (*Author*)

Looking along the Millfields Road towards Ettingshall, 1985. The first building on the left is the Spring Vale Social Club which was built in about 1941 for Stewarts & Lloyds (British Steel) workers. It was quite revolutionary at the time, having a snooker hall with up to eight full-size tables. There was also a dance hall, bars and facilities for all manner of sports. The workers here were very privileged. Next to the club was the works training centre. The large building in the centre of the picture is E.N. Wright's construction facilities, foundries and machine shops, all capable of creating the most modern blast furnaces and practically everything needed for the running and maintenance of such great works. (*Author*)

The Elisabeth furnace and the steelworks complex, 1954. The furnace, brand spanking new, soon became known as the 'Big Lizzy'. In the background the old furnaces are being taken down. (*Wolverhampton Express and Star*)

The same view today, 2001. Could anyone believe now that just over twenty years ago a great ironworks stood here, followed some eight years later by a vast open-cast site? (*Author*)

There are many scenic views of the Elisabeth standing tall and ladylike, but she was also very much a working girl. This site, now quiet and still, was where all the grafting was carried out. Her job was to turn rubbish into pure gold for her masters, and she did that well for twenty-three years. This photograph was taken in about 1978. (*Harry Eccleston*)

A last look at the Elisabeth, this time silhouetted beyond the Tarmac slag-carrying conveyor belts, 1977. This view also shows the downcomer on the right of the furnace, which carried waste gases down to ground level to be cleaned and used again as fuel. (*Author*)

The demise of the Elisabeth furnace, 11 a.m., Sunday 5 October 1980. She was blown in during December 1954 and blown out for the last time in 1977. In her lifetime it was estimated that she had produced more than 5.5 million tons of pig-iron. The felling of Elisabeth was a sad end to 200 years of iron-making in the area. Thousands flocked to see her last moments. The first charge made no impact, but then as the minutes ticked by a second charge proved lethal. She succumbed in a matter of seconds as gracefully as any lady could have wished. (*Wolverhampton Express and Star*)

A group of Stewarts & Lloyds workmen posing at the foot of the No. 4 furnace incline, *c.* 1950. Iron ore and other raw materials were carried up the incline to feed the furnace. Standing bare headed in the centre of the group is Albert Gripton. On the extreme left is Ernie Barwell, who was a winder, an important job on the furnace. He is the only one wearing a collar and tie. (*George Stevens*)

Inside the Siemens melting shop, c. 1950. Here the newly formed steel was poured into ladles then into ingots ready to be transported to the soaking pits. These were a type of furnace used for re-heating steel ingots prior to rolling. The sketch was drawn by Jim Blewitt of Ladymoor in quiet moments during his job as an overhead crane driver. The left-hand drive lorry was Canadian and was acquired soon after the Second World War. (*Jim Blewitt*)

A marvellous study by Harry Eccleston OBE of men working near the melting or open hearth furnaces, c. 1975. (*Harry Eccleston*)

A hot metal mixer furnace, *c.* 1970. It was used to hold the molten iron between the Elisabeth and the open hearth furnaces. It could hold molten metal for a number of days until it was needed. (*Harry Eccleston*)

With the Elisabeth gone it was hoped that some steel-making would continue, but by 1985 this too had come to an end. The site was cleared and by 1987 open-cast mining had begun to exploit coal reserves. This photograph shows an encounter with the unexpected – the Lanesfield Fault. The earth on the north side of the fault had collapsed into a vertical position. The fault runs from Sedgley Hill to Wednesbury. Site surveyor Paul Tomkin looks on. (*Author*)

In this view of the open-cast site in 1987 the crack in the earth is visible, running from the bottom centre of the picture to the top left-hand corner 250 million years after the earthquake that caused it. The black band in the background is the first coal seam to be encountered. It is 2 ft deep and though it looks very insignificant it was a very useful resource for the shallow miners of old. (*Author*)

Another unexpected find on the site was the base of an old furnace, and there were a lot more surprises yet to come, but the experience gained here came in useful when the workforce moved to the old Patent Shaft site at Wednesbury. This photograph was taken in 1987. (*Author*)

We cannot leave the open-cast site without mentioning the rich variety of plant fossils encountered here, including leaves, roots, tree trunks, ferns and mosses, all dating back some 300 million years. This photograph shows, top and left, small leaves known as *Neuropteris*. The slightly larger leaves are *Neuropteris gigantea*, and the larger fossil shows the imprint of a ginkgo leaf. (*Author*)

The E.N. Wright works were demolished in about 1986. This is a view from the canal bridge, showing the last vestiges of this once proud works. (*Author*)

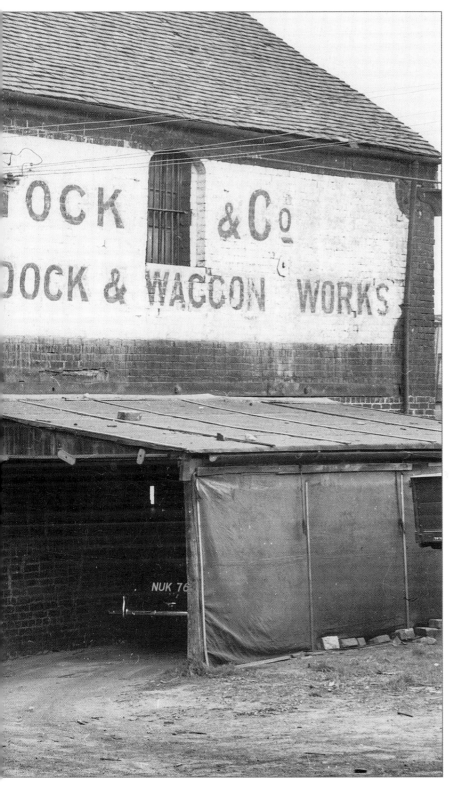

Thomas Bantock & Co.'s boat building works lay on the canal bank just north-west of the Millfields Road canal bridge. It was once a hive of activity but closed up soon after the Second World War. The Bantocks were a force to be reckoned with for many years in connection with both the canal and the Great Western Railway. The noted Bantock House Museum at Merridale was their residence. The car in the makeshift garage appears to be a Morris Minor, which dates the picture to the 1950s. (*Michael Hale Collection*)

Thomas Bantock, a central figure in the life of Wolverhampton town and also a leading light in the Queen Street Congregational Church. He came to Wolverhampton in 1849 from Golspie in Scotland. He died in 1896 and from then his rather large family continued with the business. (*Henry Arthur May*)

2

Bradley

By the 1780s John Wilkinson's iron industry in Bradley and elsewhere was really taking off, and as coins of the realm were in short supply for both his workers and tradesmen, he requested Matthew Bolton to produce tokens like the top two in this picture. His effigy, however, was likened to that of King George III and the token was readily accepted. Matthew Bolton of Soho, Birmingham, also minted coins of the realm contemporary with Wilkinson's tokens. These were quite large penny and twopenny pieces known as cartwheels (bottom two coins in the picture), and the similarities between the images of John Wilkinson and George III are clear. Until the early 1940s pipe smokers used these coins to weigh out either a penny or twopenny worth of cut tobacco. (*Author*)

A rare glimpse of industrial Bradley in 1863, showing the California Ironworks of Samuel Groucutt & Sons. The works stood on the north-west corner of Bankfield Glasshouse canal bridge. It contained eight mills and forges and forty-five puddling furnaces, the reddish cinder from which is still visible, forming an embankment at the rear of the works. (*Ben Edginton*)

The only feature remaining of the Groucutt industrial scene is the Glasshouse Bridge, which is a replacement for the one that stood there in 1863, and the footings of the footbridge seen in the foreground of the picture at the top of the page. A collapsed iron fence now lies on top of the old approach to the bridge. (*Author*)

The rolling department at Greenway's Works, 1947. The man with the tongs grappling with the metal sheet as it passes through the rolls is Harold Wootton. The works were also popularly known as The Cali because of the nearby pub called The California. (*Arthur Wootton*)

As this advertisement from about 1960 shows, Greenway's was capable of producing many types of finish on its sheet metal products. However, soon after this advertisement appeared the works ceased production. (*Bilston Handbook*)

Christmas at Top Sankey's, *c.* 1955. Among the ladies celebrating here are, back row, left to right: Gladys Bills, Pat Maydew, -?-, -?-, -?-, -?-, Dora Beards, Lilian Harris. Front row: Lilian White, Iris Skinner, -?-. (*Joan Davies*)

A Top Sankey day trip in the 1930s or 1940s. The event was brightened up by two local characters, though only one is named – William (Bill) Nash is kneeling bottom right and wearing a top hat. The man at the centre of the back row wearing a light cap is Herbert (Bert) Turner senior. The gentleman standing behind the kneeling parson and holding a bottle is Mr Morris. Mr Pearson is wearing a dark suit and is standing in the centre of the group just below the Don Everalls coach sign. (*Ron Davies Collection*)

John Toole was a leading and popular Bradley coal merchant, who had his wharf to the south of Pothouse canal bridge. During the decline of coal trade in the 1960s John said goodbye to coal and took over the popular Mount Hotel in Tettenhall. (*Bilston Handbook*)

Staff from J. Norton & Son of Loxdale Street enjoying a staff party at none other than John Toole's Mount Hotel in Tettenhall, 1970s. Norton's dealt with all manner of scrap metals. It was founded in the early 1930s but ceased trading in 1999. Left to right: Mrs Owen, -?-, -?-, -?-, D. Holmes, Nell Meacher, Dot Slaney, Lil Griffiths, Ted Griffiths, Val Pinnock, Tom Meacher and Pat Daniels. (*Dot Slaney*)

Bradley marathons were certainly popular. This crowded scene shows runner George Stevens coming up towards Pothouse Bridge. Luckily there was little traffic about in 1953. (*George Stevens*)

The marathon runners passing through Salop Street were watched not by crowds but by multitudes! On the right of the picture is The Star and Garter pub and in the centre is The Royal Oak, better known as The Long Pull. In the crowd on the right, seen holding a toddler, is Clare Stevens and the bare-headed man directly beneath the Star and Garter sign and behind the little man wearing a light cap is George Stevens senior. (*George Stevens*)

The same marathon in virtually the same spot but showing a lone runner. Note the pick-up truck. (*George Stevens*)

The winner of the 1953 Bradley marathon, proudly holding the winner's shield, was local hero of the day, George Stevens. George won the Bradley marathon twice but declined to participate in other races, believing he was unfair competition. (*George Stevens*)

A rare view of The Forum cinema before it was turned into a bingo hall and later a snooker hall. It was first known as The Queens and was built in the early 1920s by Messrs Crewe of Dudley. The first show began at 6.30 p.m. on 17 October 1921, and was *Shoulder Arms* starring Charlie Chaplin. Also on the bill were the news and a serial. Seat prices then were 5*d*, 9*d* and 1*s*. There were 600 seats, all upholstered, though most were described as 'simple benches'. There was a balconette at the rear with 1*s* seats. The first proprietor was an Ernest Hall but towards the end of the '20s the cinema was sold to Wood's Picture Halls. Sound equipment was installed, and the seating was altered and reduced to 350. In 1936 the cinema was leased to Cyril Joseph who built a new foyer and renamed the picture house The Forum. Joseph's lease expired in 1957 and the cinema was then acquired by Mr and Mrs Woodroffe. By the time they retired in the early 1970s bingo had completely taken over from the film. The film showing when the photograph was taken was *The Red Beret* starring Alan Ladd; it was made in colour in 1953. It is believed the last film shown here was *Blue Skies* starring Bing Crosby and Fred Astair. The building seen jutting out on the corner of Wright Street was a sweet shop owned by Miss Alice Davies. (*Mr and Mrs K. Woodroffe*)

Older generations can only sigh and shrug their shoulders when they see scenes such as this one looking north down Bank Street, *c.* 1960. They might remember names such as Dicky Bird, the cobbler, who had the shop on the right. Next door was a hairdressers followed by Udall's, the butchers, and then The Crown Inn. The end building housed a cook shop, where goodies such as faggots and peas were a Friday speciality. There was never one act of vandalism to spoil the old village. (*Jack Smith*)

Another scene to bring out the nostalgia, this is Bank Street looking north from King Street, *c.* 1962. The first shop on the right was Bennett's butchers, then two houses followed by Miss Cooper's grocery shop. The shop sticking out into the road was Smith's greengrocery. The Smith family also ran coaches. The shop on the left of the road with the awning was the Army and Navy Stores-cum-pawnshop. Field Street was beyond and on the left of the picture was the post office. (*Jack Smith*)

Bradley is quite a long way from the sea but that did not stop T. Hodson & Son trying to drum up a little more trade. They were also local housing agents and were responsible for building bungalows in the area, for example in Bradley Lane. (*Jack Braddock*)

St Martin's church parade, Bank Street, *c.* 1960. The Crown and Cushion pub is in the background. Leading the parade and carrying the cross is John Smith. (*Jack Smith*)

Customers enjoying a glass of ale in the back yard of The Crown and Cushion, *c.* 1960. The lady on the extreme left was landlady Elsie Yeoman. Note the handy facilities in the background. (*Ron Davies Collection*)

A happy group of Crown and Cushion customers enjoying a Sunday morning outing, or breakfast as it was known, probably at Ironbridge, *c.* 1958. The Tontine Hotel was always a favourite destination. One recognisable character at the front of the crowd lying down was local walker Tom (Jotter) Perrins. Other faces in the crowd include Harry Barratt, Jack Richards and George Selman. The coaches in the background belonged to Bradley firm Smith's. (*Ron Davies Collection*)

Probably the same Sunday morning breakfast at Ironbridge, with the Loadcroft wharf warehouse in the background. Jotter Perrins is about to set off on one of his noted walks, ably assisted by two wags – Galla Vaughan on the left and Bill Nash on the right. (*Ron Davies Collection*)

Another Sunday morning breakfast trip from the Crown and Cushion, *c.* 1960. There are lots of well-known faces but names are difficult to come by. (*Ron Davies Collection*)

A seaside trip to Blackpool from the Niagara Foundry sees this happy group posing on the steps to the beach, *c.* 1950. Among those pictured are Mrs Ratcliffe (extreme top right), Isaiah Martin (fourth row, left), Joe Thompson (right, wearing a cap), and Dolly Clarke and Brenda Nicholls (front row, fourth and fifth from the left). (*Ray Clarke*)

1994 was a special year for former pupils who attended St Martin's School in the 1930s. Two re-unions were organised by Iris Hazelhurst (née Venton) and Horace Butler, and held at their old school, now St Martin's Church Centre. Above, back row, left to right: Maud Jeffreys, William Horne, Bert Haywood, Eli Hatton, Joan Beards, John Coates and Horace Butler. Front row: Peggy Boucher, Irene Rolfe, Netta Tinsley, Dorothy Morgan, Iris Hazelhurst, Irene Clayton and Jack Davies. Below, back row: Muriel Boden, David Rickuss, Joan Walton and far right in the shadow, John Coates. Front row: Netta Tinsley, Brenda Morris, Jean Betteley, Ann Groucutt, Violet Windmill, Iris Hazelhurst, Bert Haywood and Irene Rolfe. (*Horace Butler*)

The juniors of St Martin's school trusting their agility on a rather flimsy climbing frame. *c.* 1955. On the left is David Horton and the boy with his head above the rest is Keith Stevens. The teacher is Mr Arnold. In the background is St Martin's Terrace. Even though the houses, known as Church Villas, appear to be in fair condition, they, like the rest of old Bradley, were condemned. Also missing from the scene today is the old cinder wall. One would be hard pressed to find another in the area; they were part of our local heritage and should have been preserved. (*George Stevens*)

A St Martin's School group, *c.* 1928. The walls of St Martin's Church are in the background and a little of old Slater Street is visible on the right of the picture. At the far right of the back row is Bill Evans. Second row, left to right: E. Fletcher, M. Bryan, -?-, -?-, -?-, ? Watkins, -?-, -?-, E. Barker, -?-. Third row far left, Joe Wellings. Front row, fifth from the left, Albert Gripton. (*George Stevens*)

This was perhaps the most scenic view of St Martin's Church, which was demolished in 1978. It was taken from King Street in 1950. Note also the old vicarage in the background. New bungalows and a newer vicarage now occupy the site. (*Brenda C. Beech*)

This picture of St Martin's Church complex was gleaned from the church's 1968 anniversary magazine celebrating its 100th year. It is a view from the east, showing the former vicarage on the left, with the school, now the Church Centre, on the right. The drawing was by former Headmaster Mr H.R. Arnold.

A rare view of St Martin's choir in full voice, *c. 1956*. The tall figure on the left is Bill Perkins. Immediately behind him is Bill Grinsell. On the right are the Revd Dentith and John Grinsell. (*Donated by Brenda C. Beech; photograph by A. Fellows*)

St Martin's junior choir, *c. 1939*. The choir was about to parade around the village to appeal for donations to pay for the restoration of rotting timbers discovered in the church's steeple. Leading the appeal and bearing the cross is Harry Martin and carrying the appeal banner at the rear is Bill Perkins. The boys in the right-hand row are, left to right: Geoff Butler, Bill Hill, -?-, -?-, Darren Churms, Fred Shorthouse, ? Butler and Ken Parker. Left-hand row: Barry Nash, -?-, Ken Vaughan, Donald Moore, -?-, Gordon Lavender and Howard Jeffreys. The Girls' Pipe Band marches behind. (*Harry Martin*)

In 1947 Paul Taylor of Loughborough recast St Martin's ring of eight from its old bells. The old ones weighed 75cwt, and the new just 50cwt; they cost £1,336. It would appear that in 1954 the bell pictured here had developed a flaw and required attention. Standing and watching apprehensively in the background is the verger Richard Reynolds. (*Ricky Reynolds*)

It is doubtful whether there were many military-type weddings carried out at St Martin's Church, but here in 1945 local girl Brenda Morris, who was a WAAF stationed at Half Penny Green Airfield, married a Royal Canadian Air Force pilot, Flying Officer Norman Hill, a direct descendant of Sir Roland Hill, who in 1840 initiated the Penny Post. (*Brenda C. Beech*)

Young St Martin's parishioners outside the old vicarage, 1924. The figure seated on the front row wearing a mortar-board is the Revd C.O. Haden, and centre, back row is Edith Baker. The vicar wore the mortar-board as part of his everyday dress. It is difficult to know the reason for the fancy dress turnout. The back rows have a Grecian look, but on the extreme right a bearded figure carries a scythe and just in front a lad is wearing Dickensian, Oliver Twist-type garb. On the front rows, the girls are wearing flowery head bands and seem to represent May time. (*St Martin's Church*)

Confirmation service, 7 April 1955. Left to right: Richard Reynolds (Verger), Dr Arthur Stretton Reese, Lord Bishop of Lichfield, Abraham Hartill (Vicar's Warden), the Revd Edwin A. Dentith (Vicar of St Martin's), and Richard Buxton JP (Deputising People's Warden). (*St Martin's Church*)

The Church Lads' and Girls' Brigade of St Martin's, 1994. Back row, left to right: David Brumwell, Revd Richard Walker, Peter Moore, -?-, Ian Spooner, -?-, Paul Goslin, Mark Goslin, Stephen Robinson, Mitch Hall, Ian Grennan and Tony Yates. Second row: Betty Thomas, Martine Brumwell, -?-, Karen Robinson, Naomi Withers, Rebecca Edkins, Alison Siverns, Stacey Jeavons, Clare Spooner, Gemma Jarvis, Celia Walker and Kirsty Hall. Front row: -?-, -?-, Dominic Smith, Benjamin O'Brian and Lauren Childs. The names of those in third and fourth rows are not known. (*St Martin's Church*)

Once in a blue moon a picture of a whole congregation is taken. This one shows the vibrant community of St Martin's Church Centre (based in the old St Martin's School) on Sunday 8 October 2000. Among the faces you will find Ethel Boden, Ian Spooner, Ruth Jones, Celia Walker, Mr and Mrs Tony Yates, Rosemary Preston, John Lloyd, Rick Reynolds, Iris Pardon, Margaret Corbett, Frank Venton, Daniel Thompson, Bethany Thompson, Iris Hazelhurst, Grace Preston, Joan Oram, Mary Stanford, David Brumwell, Jody Paskin, Freda Yates, Charmaine Bailey, Kamela Jassic, Lilian Hill, Ruth Hill, Terry and Pauline Calloway, Jean Sneyd, Mr and Mrs W.E. Potts, Mrs Matthews and Mavis Johnson. (*Revd Richard Walker*)

Bradley scouts on parade in Slater Street, *c.* 1950. The scout leader was John Richards. At that time the street was mainly dominated by St Martin's School and the Buxton family's business. The building with the posters was Buxton's sweets and general shop and next door was Richard Buxton's offices, with his sheet metal and engineering works alongside. (*Jack Smith*)

Another scouts parade in Slater Street, this time outside the Buxton works in about 1961. (*Jack Smith*)

A children's Christmas party at the Crown and Cushion pub, *c.* 1956. To the left of centre is the Revd E.A. Dentith. The tall girl on the back row wearing a dark coat is Yvonne Clarke (née Selman). (*Ray Clarke*)

Alderman Fred Ledsam, Mayor of Wolverhampton, is seen posing with Mrs Brenda Beech and her daughter Pam, both from Canada. Brenda, formerly from Bradley, was persuaded by Fred to try on the Mayoral Robes; they fitted perfectly and she looked every inch a potential Mayoress. (*Brenda C. Beech*)

Thomas Price of King Street was a clever engineer who made working model steam engines. This photograph shows him at the age of seventy-nine in 1965 posing by one of his horizontal models. A caption on the engine says, 'Oil me well and keep me clean and I will work with little steam'. (*Evelyn Thomas*)

Church Terrace, King Street, *c.* 1941. Note the sand bags piled up. In the background is the hazy form of Baker's sweet shop in King Street. Back row, left to right: Bill Cole, Dot Wilde and PC Bill Burgess. Front row: little Elaine Burgess, William Henry Burgess, Natalie Burgess, Elizabeth Burgess. (*Arthur Wootton*)

This photograph shows Bradley people out on a trip, probably organised by Mrs Smith of Bank Street greengrocery for her regular customers. On the back row in the dark coat is Mrs Hallmark, who also had a greengrocery and later a newsagents in Cross Street. Second from the left on the front row, is Mrs Smith who has a glass in her hand. The photograph was taken in about 1956. (*Arthur Wootton*)

Bank Street looking north from Lord Street and Jordan Place, *c.* 1957. The sign for the Swan Inn is on the extreme left. The house on the right beyond the Jordan Place sign was the home of the Heighway family, who in former days were dairy farmers. The Crown and Cushion public house lies on the left between the second and third street lights. (*Jack Smith*)

William and Elizabeth Wootton outside their home in Crane Road with their grandson Raymond, *c.* 1937. The blocks used to build the house were made from material from the Wilkinson slag heap. (*Arthur Wootton*)

A cuddle in the garden at 7 Martin Road – Tom Morris and little Brenda Morris with her dolly June, *c.* 1926. (*Brenda C. Beech*)

An early view of the Swan Inn, probably dating from before the First World War. It was a time when the Jeavons family were landlords, he taking charge of the main bar and she, Betsy, the outdoor sales. The young lady with babe in her arms is almost certainly their daughter. The other people in the picture are probably customers. Note the clock on the tram pole, telling the time of the next tram. This was normally set by the outgoing tram conductor. (*Jack Braddock*)

A bleak wintery view of the Swan Inn and the houses adjoining it just before the demolition teams moved in, *c.* 1965. The Niagara foundry was situated at the end of the buildings and next to it was the park with the Memorial Cross which can be seen in the distance. (*Jack Smith*)

In about 1967 the senior citizens of Bradley and district gathered in Coronation Park to highlight their need for a building to hold their meetings. They organised many fund-raising events and all the hard work was rewarded on 20 March 1971 when Bradley Senior Citizens' Centre was declared open by Councillor Dennis Turner on behalf of the Bradley Trust Committee. (*Wolverhampton Express and Star*)

Around Bradley Memorial Cross, the Guides, Scouts and choir and congregation of St Martin's Church gather at Armistice time to say prayers for the many from this village who never returned from the horrors of the First World War. Leading this service in 1935 is the Revd Charles Oliver Haden. Richard Reynolds is holding the cross. (*Ricky Reynolds*)

Bradley from the Coronation Park, *c.* 1960. The houses on the right of the picture still remain, but sadly the church has gone and so has the pool, which was a delight to the local children who came to paddle and fish for sticklebacks and tadpoles. (*Jack Smith*)

Coronation Park, the bandstand and the Royal British Legion Club, *c.* 1960. Note the backs of the old houses in Lord Street and Hill Street. The bandstand, or banner as it was known, was a popular venue for brass bands and a summer Sunday evening's musical repertoire was rarely missed. How long would the benches last in this day and age? (*Jack Smith*)

A sketch of Bradley Memorial Hall that never was, *c.* 1950. After the Second World War the worthies of Bradley planned that the village should have a community hall to be proud of, but the project proved to be too ambitious and the cash never materialised. (*Jack Braddock*)

Members of the guilds at St Martin, St Agnes and St Catherine parading in Wilkinson Avenue, *c.* 1950. Miss Skinner is on the footpath between the first two banners, and Mrs Layland is immediately behind the last girl in white. (*Ron Davies Collection*)

Mildred Beards posing in her ARP (Air Raid
Precautions) uniform outside her home in Wilkinson
Avenue, c. 1941. (*Joan Davies*)

The slag heaps created by Wilkinson's blast furnace in
Wilkinson Avenue were a popular playground for local
children. They were known as The Rocks. The two
children at the back are twins Jimmy (left) and Philip
Boylin. In front of them are Becky Gripton (née Perks),
Barbara Taylor and Jean Perks. The trouble with
playing on slag heaps was that if you got cut, it
usually, as they said, 'Went bad ways.' This picture
was taken in about 1957. (*Becky Gripton*)

Anna Stevens (née York) donned her husband's uniform for this picture taken in 1915, in the Pig Hole (Adams Yard) at the lower end of Wilkinson Avenue. Her 'partner' was her sister Mary Jane. (*George Stevens*)

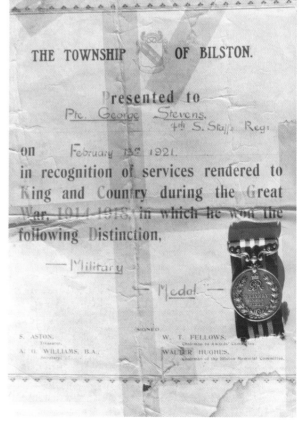

Anna Stevens' husband George, was presented with this certificate by the Township of Bilston in 1921 in recognition of services rendered during the First World War. He was awarded the Military Medal for bravery on the Flanders fields. It is the highest distinction awarded to Other Ranks after the VC. The actual medal lies on the certificate. (*George Stevens*)

Who remembers seeing this penny-ha'penny luxury cycling armchair contraption? The date is 1939 and George Stevens is doing a balancing act in his back garden in Pugh Road. The bicycle somehow came into the hands of one Arthur Lloyd of The Rolling Mill pub in Highfields Road, who continued to use it during the early 1940s. (*George Stevens*)

Same bike, same garden but trying her luck is George's sister, Bett. (*George Stevens*)

Still in the same garden in Pugh Road. This time it is about 1941 and George Stevens has been called to duty in Sankey's Home Guard. With him is Bill Butler. The pit mound in the background is part of Coronation Park and on top of it is the War Memorial. (*George Stevens*)

Three Bradley stalwarts on a trip to Blackpool, 1940. Left to right: Tom Stokes, Arthur Weekes and Harold Wootton. Arthur was a popular publican of The Rolling Mill in Millfields Road, Bilston, from the 1930s to the 1950s. (*Arthur Wootton*)

A Smith's conducted tour, 1936. In the coach doorway is Ted Philips, then from left to right: Mr Wootton, J. Fellows, -?-, -?-, -?-, Fred Smith (with thumb in waistcoat armpit, a once popular pose), Bill Clark, -?-, -?-, Mr Capewell (with the moustache), -?-, -?-, -?-, Mr Cole (smoking a pipe), -?- and, squatting at the front, H. Wootton. (*Arthur Wootton*)

A group of Bradley ladies on holiday in Blackpool from The Bird in Hand pub in Hill Street, *c.* 1938. Back row, left to right: -?-, Mrs Beech, -?-, Mrs Harris, Mrs Braine, Mrs Ward, -?-, Mrs Richards. Middle row: Mrs Evans, -?-, Mrs Mitton, Mrs Smith, Mrs Philpots, Mrs Bryan. Front row: -?-, Mrs Tinsley, Mrs Shorthouse, -?-, -?-, Mrs Richards, -?-. The names of the two women in the doorway are not known. (*Arthur Wootton*)

Two long-established Bradley doctors, Charles Slim and his wife Kathleen, affectionately known as Lady Slim, 1935. (*David Horton*)

A younger Dr Slim with his brother, later Viscount Field Marshal William Slim, who occasionally visited Bradley. Field Marshal Slim was commander of the so-called Forgotten Army in Burma. After the Second World War he became Governor General of Australia from 1953–1960. When he visited Bradley soon after 1946, the locals put out bunting and streamers in his honour. (*David Horton*)

Drs Slim at their retirement home at Crossways, Bittadon, near Barnstaple, North Devon, *c.* 1955. It was Christmas Day, and weren't they lucky geese. (*David Horton*)

Jim Horton posing by the sign for Slim Avenue, *c.* 1960. The Hortons were great friends of the Slims and often visited them in their retirement years. Bill was a master tailor and took great care that Dr Slim was always well dressed. After the death of his wife Dr Slim went to live with his son in New Zealand. (*David Horton*)

Bradley carnival, Lord Street, *c.* 1949. In the background to the left is the Daisy Bank School annex in Lane Street. In the centre are Barnsley's offices and on the right is the rear of Lane's electrical shop. The girl on the extreme left of the picture is Eileen Cox, and the girl surrounded by a crowd of boys is Elsie Reynolds. Immediately behind her is a young Dennis Turner. Benny Shepherd is in academic robes and the parson is William (Bill) Nash. Third from the right is Ernie Johnson (now residing in Germany) and on the bicycle is Norman Davies. (*Walker and Wootton*)

Bradley carnival Lord Street, 1950. There are lots of familiar faces but names are difficult to pinpoint. However on the extreme right of the picture, wearing a cap, is Mr Caddick. (*Walker and Wootton*)

The Globe public house in Ash Street, *c*. 1980. At one time there were no fewer than six pubs within the vicinity of Ash Street, and The Globe was at the very centre. The building remains and is now used as offices. (*Arthur Wootton*)

Ann Wood leading her Cub troop along Ash Street, *c*. 1960. The cinder wall has now vanished, and so has Henshaw's DIY premises, along with the old houses. Note the large complex in the background that was once Perry's foundry. (*Jack Braddock*)

A group of Daisy Bank scholars, *c.* 1925. Their teacher, Arthur Hale, is at top left. On the front row, far right is Tom Russell. (*Arthur Wootton*)

Relaxing after a hectic Bradley gala day, 1997. Gala Queen for the day, Stephanie Bateman, sits in front of the wall with her attendant. (*Arthur Wootton*)

Bradley Resources Action Group (BRAG) organises and runs the annual Rose Queen, Prince and Princess competition. BRAG also supports and helps Daisy Bank Community Centre with the organisation and running of the events and procession on Gala Day, which took place on 14 July in 2001. BRAG members Kath Mason and John Ansell took the photographs to capture the day, lorries and drivers were donated by local haulage firms Starr Roadways, Vulcan Road, Bilston, and R.K. Transport, Willenhall. Bradley Gala Rose Queen was Maria Peake, first attendant, Lucy Sambrookes, second attendant, Kirsty Cooper, Senior Prince, Anthony Gibbons, Senior Princess, Samantha Ellis, Junior Prince, Luke Timbrell, Junior Princess, Hayley Gibbons. Others on the float are second and third place runners up. (*Kath Mason and John Ansell*)

A Western scene from the Gala including back row, left to right: Alan Wright and Gary Ellis. Front row: Karl Russon, Wendy Groucutt, Amy Dean, -?-, Charlotte Lewis and Johnathon Gibbons. Sitting: Lucy Parton and Jennifer Wright. (*Kath Mason and John Ansell*)

The Primitive Methodist Chapel in Hall Green Street stood more or less on the site of the present medical centre. In its day it had a vibrant little congregation, but when the old premises were cleared out during the 1960s, its community was dispersed to all quarters of both the Coseley and the Bilston districts. With no congregation the building was downgraded to industrial uses. (*Author*)

The medical centre in Hall Green Street. This is the home of Dr Chaman Lal's practice and without doubt it is a great credit to the community of Bradley. It was officially opened by Dennis Turner, MP for Wolverhampton South-East, on Thursday 5 January 1995. (*Author*)

For the official opening of the new medical centre, Dr Lal, left, was joined by local dignitaries, left to right: Councillor Bert Turner, Councillor Norman Davies OBE (Leader of the Council) and Dennis Turner MP. (*Dr Chaman Lal*)

Dr Lal brings his staff together in 1994 to explain the layout of the new surgery. Listening intently are, back row, left to right: John Guest, Kate Guest and Savita Kainth. Front row: Pauline Powell and Carol Pickerill. (*Bradley Medical Centre*)

This handsome towered building of terracotta built in the Gothic style was the Wesleyan Chapel in Hall Green Street just before its demolition in 1979. It was built in 1902 to the plans of Wednesbury architect Charles William Davies Joynson at a cost of £4,500. (*Author*)

Twenty years after the demolition of the old chapel, this newer but smaller chapel now stands on the site. (*Author*)

The Wesleyan school building, 1949. Note the three ornate dormer gables. (*Arthur Wootton*)

This is the same building in 2000, but now showing its age. The dormer gables are now gone. However, the building is still very much in use for various functions. (*Author*)

Wesleyan Chapel anniversary, 1938. Unfortunately there are far too many people in the picture to name them all, but it does include, on the back row, Jack Woodyatt, Jack Ruby, Tom Russell and John Grinsell. The gentleman in front on the left is Charles Lathe and on the right at the front is George Davies. Also present is Elija Bailly. Among the ladies are Mary Bailly, Vi Grainger (née Fletcher), Norma Turton, Mary Turton and Edna Davies. (*Vi Grainger*)

The Wesleyan choir in full voice, 1974. Back row, left to right: Joe Hall, Jack Cartwright, David Jeavons, Barry Oliver, John Grinsell and Mr Dolman. Among the ladies are Lily Darby, Mrs Churms and Muriel Evans. In the second row, second from the left is Margaret Thomas (née Grainger) and immediately in front of her is her daughter Louise. (*Vi Grainger*)

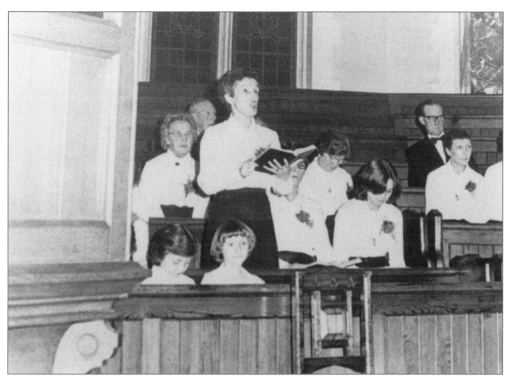

Soprano Margaret Thomas performing a solo with the Wesleyan choir, 1974. (*Vi Grainger*)

Choirmaster Mr Coulson on the left, Aubrey Evans and Mrs Coulson, *c.* 1976. Mr and Mrs Coulson are being honoured for their work with the choir. The tankard on the table was presented to Mr Coulson. Vi Grainger is the middle one of the three ladies watching. (*Bob Lathe*)

Len Weaver makes a presentation to Evelyn Smith and Alice Taylor for their long association with the Wesleyan chapel, *c.* 1976. Aubrey Evans watches over the ceremony. (*Bob Lathe*)

A Wesleyan school pantomime group, *c.* 1920. Second row down, left to right: Sid Parks (immediately behind the clown), Ian Thomas, and Rene Boyd. (*Arthur Wootton*)

These days it is hard to believe there was ever a graveyard attached to the Wesleyan chapel, but here to prove it is little David Woodyatt sitting on one of the old gravestones, *c.* 1951. (*Arthur Wootton*)

A gala at the rear of the Wesleyan Chapel, *c.* 1970. For many years the land had been used as allotments, and during the Second World War pigs were reared here – a necessary food supply. The idea of reviving the allotments was reintroduced a decade or so ago with some success but today the area is used for a little gardening. (*Arthur Wootton*)

A Wesleyan chapel trip, *c*. 1930. Among the faces are Mrs Maria Lewis, Mrs Bunce, Mrs Woodyatt, Mrs Smith, Alice Taylor, Mrs Harper, Mrs Thomas, Mrs Gillard, Mrs Green, Mrs Dyson, Mrs Morris, Mrs Higgs, Elsie Russell, Mrs Brace, Mrs Gillard, Hilda Smith, Edna Boyd, Evelyn Smith and Marjorie Brace. (*Arthur Wootton*)

This photograph from about 1935 was clearly taken at a special function but what the function was and where it took place are long forgotten. Most of the individuals here are from the Bradley district and include, front row centre, Detective Sergeant Colclough. Second row back, left to right: -?-, -?-, -?-, -?-, Mr Brown, -?-, Jack Woodyatt, -?-. Third row back, immediately behind Detective Sergeant Colclough, is Mr Fellows. (*Arthur Wootton*)

Members of the Royal Antediluvian (Before the Flood) Order of Buffaloes, or Buffs for short, outside the Britannia pub in Hall Green Street, *c.* 1925. The Order was founded in about 1875 to promote brotherhood among men and is believed to have originated at the Harp Tavern, Russell Street, Drury Lane. Back row, left to right: Arthur Griffiths, -?-, -?-, -?-, -?-, Jim Horton, Eli Davies, -?-, -?-, -?-. Second row: -?-, -?-, -?-, -?-, Bill Cole, Arthur Weekes, -?-, Galla Vaughan, -?-, Bill Ball. Front row: Arthur Caddick, -?-, -?-, -?-, -?-, Ted Lewis, -?-, -?-, -?-, Mr Whitehouse. (*Nancy Cole*)

Jack Brown, a popular publican of both Wesley Street and the Britannia pub in Hall Green Street, 1920s and '30s. (*Arthur Wootton*)

St Aidan's Mission, situated on the Big Hilly, the highest point in this district, was one of three mission halls to be built to complement Christ Church in Coseley in about 1888 by the Revd W. Spencer, a distant relative of the late Diana, Princess of Wales. All three missions were dedicated to Saxon Saints – St Aidan, St Oswald (Ladymoor) and St Cuthbert. Only the mission of St Cuthbert in Wallbrook remains. The missions were built to combat the monopoly of the Methodist influence in these areas. St Aidan's, seen here in 1960, faced Coseley parish and was in full view of Christ Church. (*Author*)

St Aidan's had a nice little choir in its day. This is one of its members, Brian Cunliffe, seen among the herbage outside the mission, *c.* 1950. (*Joan Oram*)

The former Bricklayers Arms, Brierley Lane, *c.* 1965. It is now a private residence. The pub was situated alongside the former Wolverhampton–Worcester railway. On the right a car is just approaching the bridge that once spanned the railway, but has now been levelled. In the distance is the Hilly and the buildings that once graced its ridge, possibly with St Aidan's mission among them. (*Robert Hale*)

Looking up Hall Green Street from Cross Street, *c.* 1950. The main building in the picture was Russell's newsagents. Mr Russell was also a piano teacher and it seems every child in Bradley had lessons with him. It is difficult to say how many of his pupils made the grade; it seems his strictness may have put them off. (*Author*)

Mr and Mrs Barnsley with their young daughter Bella outside their corner grocery shop in Cross Street, off Wesley Street, 1910. The sign near the top of the doorway seems to say, 'Testers for the New Safe Lamp'. (*Arthur Wootton*)

Another grocery store Cross Street, *c.* 1925. Sarah Ann Martin and her son Bert are standing in the doorway. (*Arthur Wootton*)

Inside the Greyhound, Cross Street, *c.* 1960. A few of the regulars are enjoying their favourite tipples. Sitting from left to right are Isaiah Nock, Joe Cunliffe, Bill Boden and Holly Guest. (*Joan Oram*)

Three pretty girls outside the converted stables belonging to Joe Turton, licensee of the British Oak, Wesley Street, *c.* 1960. Left to right: Linda Edge, Marion Turton and Joan Cunliffe. (*Joan Oram*)

William (Snapper) Boden counting his chickens at his home in Rose Street, *c.* 1930. William, an iron puddler, also bred bull terriers, hence the nickname Snapper. (*Joan Oram*)

This is William's wife Hannah, sitting comfortably on what looks like a homemade garden bench, *c.* 1930. There were no handy B&Q stores in those days. (*Joan Oram*)

Holden's shop, Rose Street, *c.* 1970. It was formerly a public house known as The Who Would Have Thought It? John Wilkinson's father, Isaac, said 'Who would have thought it?' whenever he invented something new, especially if it worked to his satisfaction. (*Author*)

The old canal as it looped alongside Batmans Hill Road, and as seen through the eyes of twelve-year-old Robert Baker of Ladymoor, *c.* 1922. Though the perspective of the background may not quite be true, the foreground scene is remarkably lifelike and dramatic, capturing all the despondency of those early days of recession – exceptional drawing for a boy of twelve. (*Robert Baker*)

Alf Lowe (left) and Ken Cooper outside the old offices, Matthew's Foundry, *c.* 1960. Alf was a chargehand and Ken was a maintenance carpenter. (*Les Webb*)

Another Matthews scene, this time of the moulders, *c.* 1957. This was always a spick and span factory, but it must have been a great pleasure for men just to be able to stand up at the end of a long day. (*Edward Matthews Ltd*)

These customers have found a cosy corner to enjoy a tipple and a natter in the Old Bush, Cross Street, *c.* 1950. Back row, left to right: ? Hill, Steve Johnson, -?-, Bob Slaney (standing), -?-. Front row: ? Johnson and Tom Bethel. (*Dot Slaney*)

There never seemed to be many children in Bradley Lane during the mid-1950s, but here are three of them in about 1956 acting out their fantasies in a military fashion. Left to right: Alan Amos, Tony Slaney and Michael Shiels. (*Don Slaney*)

British Waterways yard, Bradley Lane, showing some outsize replicas of traditional boat folk utensils prepared for an exhibition boat rally at Chester, *c.* 1995. Note the ubiquitous castle and roses scenes. The artist has his back to us and the person looking on is Joe Holinshead. (*Author*)

A wintery scene down on the canal at British Waterways yard, Bradley Lane. The occasion was the launch of a restored tug boat, and here are the lads responsible for carrying out the work between 1970 and 1975. Left to right: Bill Harwood (Foreman), Cliff Sherwood, Tony Druce, Jeff Jenkins, Chris Bant, Bob Cartwright, Frank Williams, Brian Onions, John Williamson and Gordon Butler. (*Bob Cartwright, British Waterways*)

The passenger rail service between Wolverhampton Low Level and Birmingham Snow Hill was always a popular commuting line, and one wonders why Lord Beeching decided that it should be closed. Thirty years or so on it was resurrected in the shape of the Metro, which in spite of the numerous setbacks has proved more successful than anyone had dared to hope. Today the service is regular, fast, clean and much quieter than the huge steam locomotives of old and the diesel engines that followed them. This is the Bradley Lane stop. (*Author*)

Standing quite alone, in what was a wilderness up until the mid-1930s is the former Fiery Holes tollhouse. The architecture of the building appears to be a mixture of both Gothic and Classical styles. The doorway has a Gothic arch and both the windows and doorway have label mouldings or dripstones, another Gothic feature. The dentiled eaves are Classical. The Wilkinson's furnace was once at the bottom of its garden. (*Ron Davies Collection*)

This was the type of ticket obtained at various tollhouses in order to travel the roads in the area. (*Author*)

3

Ladymoor

Tips, embankments and pit mounds are symbols of Ladymoor more than any other town or village in the locality. No image catches the mood better than this semi-silhouetted study by Harry Eccleston from about 1960. Perhaps the years of tipping furnace waste here was all to the good – the Black Country Route now passes over this particular site. (*Harry Eccleston*)

This sturdy building, the Wagon and Horses in Moor Street, like the Hope Pole and Union mentioned earlier, was to end its days in isolation. Of the six public houses that once flourished here, only one now remains, namely The George and Dragon. This photograph was taken in about 1970. (*Ron Arnold*)

Landlady Nancy Wood in the doorway of the Wagon and Horses, *c.* 1977. With her is Joan Arnold (née Elwell), an original village girl. (*Ron Arnold*)

Just beyond the Wagon and Horses in Moor Street was Dugmore's coal merchants. This is the founder of the firm, William H. Dugmore, with his grandson Graham beside his coal lorry in about 1956. (*Harold Dugmore*)

Two of William's sons, Harold (left) and Ron, *c.* 1956. The lorry was their pride and joy and was acquired after many years of working with horse and cart. (*Harold Dugmore*)

Another of William's sons, this is Arthur with his little relative, Jan Van De Sande, again by the lorry, which incidentally was a Morris Commercial. (*Harold Dugmore*)

Ladymoor had its share of cot buildings. This one in Moor Street was the home of John Van De Sande and family. John, a Dutchman who was stationed at Wrottesley during the Second World War, married a local girl and settled here, though the family have since returned to Holland. The photograph was taken in about 1956. (*Harold Dugmore*)

When young Robert Baker looked out of his bedroom window in Withy Lane, this is the scene that met his eyes, *c.* 1930. Night scenes such as this of the Spring Vale steelworks were always an awe-inspiring sight. Sketched in crayon, the picture shows the view looking north from Withy Lane. The works railway bridge over the old road from Bilston to Coseley is plain to see. (*Robert Baker*)

Robert Baker was to achieve a certain fame in ceramics and earned the title Professor, first with Wedgwood, then with Royal Worcester porcelain. His Evesham ware, shown here, is still popular today. He was once given the task of re-creating medieval floor tiles for Winchester Cathedral to replace worn and missing ones. To do this he built his own replica medieval kiln. At Wood Green on the edge of the New Forest between 1930 and 1931 he and fellow post-graduate student Edward Payne created no fewer than fifty murals of the village life for the new village hall. In retirement with his talented wife, Eve, he set about restoring medieval church wall paintings in various parts of the country. (*Author*)

Broadlanes Methodist Chapel in its heyday. It was built in 1903 to replace the old Ladymoor chapel which had fallen victim of mining subsidence, but by 1976 it had been taken down in the general slum clearance in the area. Its important brass plaques now hang in Sedgley Museum in Brick Street. An elm tree marks its site near Withy Lane. (*Author*)

On the opposite side of the road to the site of the chapel and in a sunken plot lies this old cot, for many years the home of the Kyte family. In years gone by Mr Kyte seems to have been a coffin maker, which would make sense as a funeral director lived but 100 yards distant next to the Ladymoor mission. Mr Kyte appears also to have been a maker of grandfather clock cabinets. He would deliver his finished work on his back. (*Author*)

The last remnant of what were once the noted but gloomy four bridges at Capponfield, 1985. It had been many years since the railway passed over this once busy but rough foot road, one the author used for many years, especially on his way from Ladymoor to Stonefield school. (*Author*)

This old corner wall was the last remnant of the Capponfield furnace site. Photographed in 1980, it reveals the art of bricklayers of old who used any available materials to maintain walls. This one was made up of ordinary house bricks, cinder or slag, local stone and furnace fire-bricks. (*Author*)

Mr and Mrs Ernest and Ethel Bateman on the corner wall of their garden, Capponfield, *c.* 1948. The wall behind them was the furnace boundary, and part of the old road from Bilston to Coseley is clearly visible. (*Alec Bateman*)

A Bateman get together, *c.* 1948. Back row, left to right: Gwen, daughter-in-law Mary, Mrs Bateman, Dorothy, and Vera with baby Margaret. Middle row: granddaughters Sheila, Lorraine and Ann. Front row: June, Mr Bateman and Joan. June and Joan are twins. (*Alec Bateman*)

The one-sided open structure of the railway bridge as it rather awkwardly spans the canal at Capponfield Stop, which is seen just beyond the bridge, 1946. At this point the canal narrows to the width of one boat. Here the stop-keeper, who lived in a house close by, would measure the tonnage of a boat's contents. It was also a place where a plank of wood was placed across the stop to give access to and from Capponfield and Bradley – an experience something like walking a tightrope! (*Alec Bateman*)

When the Capponfield furnaces were blown out for the last time in about 1929, the working boats in the works canal basin also fell victim to the times. Neglected, they soon filled with water and partly submerged in the basin which became a watery graveyard. This shows the scene in 1946. (*Harry Eccleston*)

A sketch of the Brickmaker's Arms, Ladymoor, *c.* 1928. by Andrew Barnett. Andrew's close relatives lived in the houses next to the pub. They were active Methodists and as such were completely teetotal, but appeared quite content with their situation. The Humpage family lived here afterwards for many years, followed by the Dykes and Davies family. Note the postbox in between the doorway and window of the house. (*Andrew Barnett*)

Another 1920s look at the Brickmaker's Arms, this time at the rear tea gardens – a fashion to encourage custom in those days. Isaac Fellows was the licensee of the day. (*Ron Davies Collection*)

The back of the Brickmaker's Arms, 1947. On the tricycle is the publican's grandson, Alan Davies. (*Author*)

At the back of the Brickmaker's Arms, 1947. Left to right: bar helpers Rene Davies and Violet Davies, and landlady Elizabeth Davies. (*Author*)

A side view of St Oswald's mission church, showing the wealth of cinder or furnace slag that went into making this building special. It was built in 1888 and demolished in the mid-1970s. This photograph shows the vandals have been at work. (*Author*)

Inside the mission hall, 1975. Who in the world could vandalise the font where so many Ladymoor folk were baptised? (*Author*)

Ladymoor pool, known as Hipkins's pool in earlier days, is quite the most pleasant spot in the district, harbouring a variety of waterfowl, especially swan, wild Canadian geese, moorhens, mallard ducks and coot. Other wild birds join in to feed on the bounty provided by visitors. The pool is really a swag, caused by the crowning in of mineworks. This is a 1950s scene; then only swans and moorhens were resident. The houses in the background were known as Chillington Terrace because they faced the Chillington cupola furnace near to Highfields (Boat) bridge. The houses on the extreme left, of 1937 vintage, are still with us. (*Joe Richards*)

Ladymoor resident Esther Richards and her niece Gloria by the pool on an old cast-iron pipeline that outcropped for a few yards at the pool's edge, *c.* 1958. No one seems to know where the pipe came from, where it went or its use. (*Joe Richards*)

Today Ladymoor pool is but a shadow of its former self because of an embankment created by British Waterways so that the land behind could be used to dump canal dredging waste. This is a pre-embankment view of the site taken in about 1975. (*Author*)

With its ever-changing light, the pool attracts many photographers. This shot was taken one winter's evening in about 1995 as the wild Canadian geese were marching across the ice to safety away from the marauding fox. (*Remi Hodister*)

To the south of the steelworks lay the vast tipping area. Before 1940 numerous iron pickers were to be found on its slopes, but the iron they collected was generally of poor quality and a week's picking yielded little more than 10s. One of the regulars was Mrs Nock from Daisy Bank, seen here carrying her hard-won burden on her head. She was the last of her kind in the area. She was acutely deaf and iron picking was her only form of income. (*Author*)

Looking north from the Boat Inn towards Capponfield, *c.* 1980. Members of the now defunct Bilston Conservation Association planted trees on the open land here. The exercise was a huge success for the area is now a well-established woodland. (*Author*)

The view from Highfields bridge, looking across the site of the Highfields haulage business to the steelworks and the Elisabeth in the distance, 1975. (*Author*)

Highfields canal bridge, 1925. Under the bridge and in the distance is the site of the Capponfield furnace. This part of the canal was then a main thoroughfare from this area of Coseley to Bilston. (*Andrew Barnett*)

ACKNOWLEDGEMENTS

Thanks to: John Ansell, Ron Arnold, the late Robert Baker, the late Andrew Barnett, Alec Bateman, Brenda C. Beech, Jack Bevan, Angela Bird, the late Jim Blewitt, Brian Braddock, the late Jack Braddock, Bob Cartwright, Ray Clarke, Nancy Cole, Ken Cooper, Joan Davies, Irene Duckett, Harold Dugmore, Harry N. Eccleston OBE, Ben Edginton, Vi Grainger, Becky Gripton, John Guest, Michael Hale, George Hawkins, Roy Hawthorne, Andrew Hickman, Stan Hill, Remi Hodister, David Horton, Len Hull, Dr C. Lal, Harry Martin, Kath Mason, Beryl Nash, Joan Oram, Andy Patel, Dr Rangel, Rick Reynolds, Dot Slaney, the late Jack Smith, John Smith, George Stevens, Dr Sullivan, Evelyn Thomas, Dennis Turner MP, Janet Unitt, Revd Richard and Celia Walker, Messrs Walker and Wootton Photographers, Edna Wilson, Mr and Mrs K. Woodroffe, Arthur Wootton, Ray Wootton, Cissy Woodyatt and Ron Wright. Further acknowledgements are due to the Black Country Society, staff of Wolverhampton Archives and local Studies, and staff of the *Express and Star* archives, Wolverhampton. The author is most grateful to everyone who has loaned or donated photographs, either in the past or specifically for this book. Special thanks are due to all anonymous contributors.

Every effort has been made to contact all copyright holders of photographs where copyright has not originated with the person owning them. All royalties from this book are to be donated to our most deserving Compton Hospice. The royalties from the previous book have up until September 2001 accumulated £2,600 for this cause and there will be further payments as sales continue.

BRITAIN IN OLD PHOTOGRAPHS

To order any of these titles please telephone our distributor,
Haynes Publishing, on 01963 442105
For a catalogue of these and our other titles please telephone
Joanne Govier at Sutton Publishing on 01453 732423